Basketball

Julie Murray

Abdo
SPORTS HOW TO
Kids

abdopublishing.com

Published by Abdo Kids, a division of ABDO, PO Box 398166, Minneapolis, Minnesota 55439.
Copyright © 2018 by Abdo Consulting Group, Inc. International copyrights reserved in all countries.
No part of this book may be reproduced in any form without written permission from the publisher.

Printed in the United States of America, North Mankato, Minnesota.

102017

012018

Photo Credits: Alamy, AP Images, iStock, Shutterstock

Production Contributors: Teddy Borth, Jennie Forsberg, Grace Hansen

Design Contributors: Christina Doffing, Candice Keimig, Dorothy Toth

Publisher's Cataloging in Publication Data

Names: Murray, Julie, author.

Title: Basketball / by Julie Murray.

Description: Minneapolis, Minnesota : Abdo Kids, 2018. | Series: Sports how to |
          Includes glossary, index and online resource (page 24).

Identifiers: LCCN 2017908184 | ISBN 9781532104121 (lib.bdg.) | ISBN 9781532105241 (ebook) |
          ISBN 9781532105807 (Read-to-me ebook)

Subjects: LCSH: Basketball--Juvenile literature. | Basketball--History--Juvenile literature.

Classification: DDC 796.323 --dc23

LC record available at https://lccn.loc.gov/2017908184

Table of Contents

Basketball

Ella loves basketball. She is ready to play!

5

It is played on a court. Each team has 5 players.

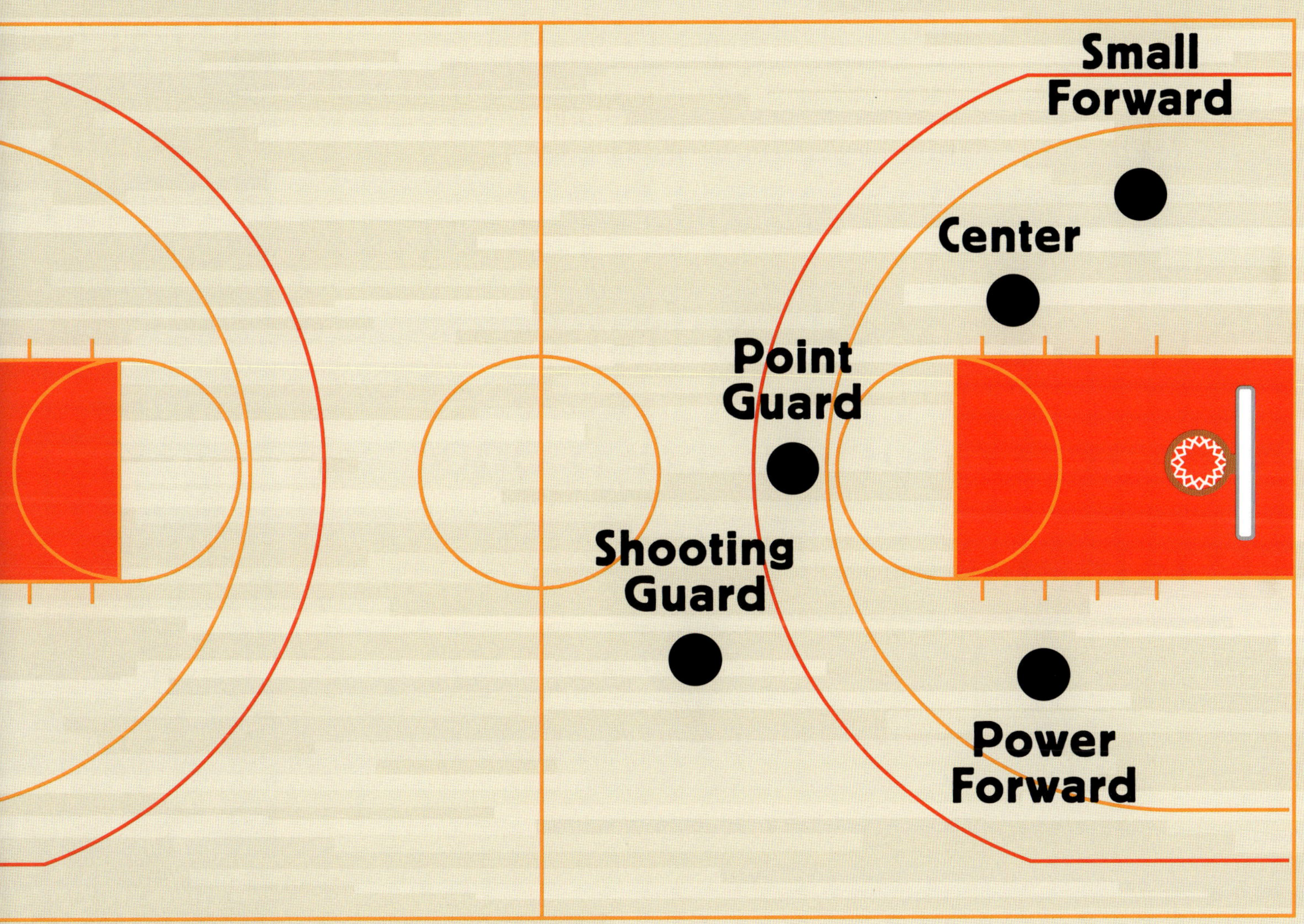

Small
Forward
Center
Point
Guard
Shooting
Guard
Power
Forward

An **NBA** game is 48 minutes. There are 4 quarters. Each one is 12 minutes.

23
2:46
24
23
37
JACK ATTACK
KEEP THE T WOLVES
UNDER 75% FREE THROW
in the box
KIA
GOLDEN STATE WARRIORS
ORACLE ARENA
ORACLE ARENA
42
30
25
13

Players cannot run with the ball. They must dribble it.

Players can pass the ball.

Chad catches it.

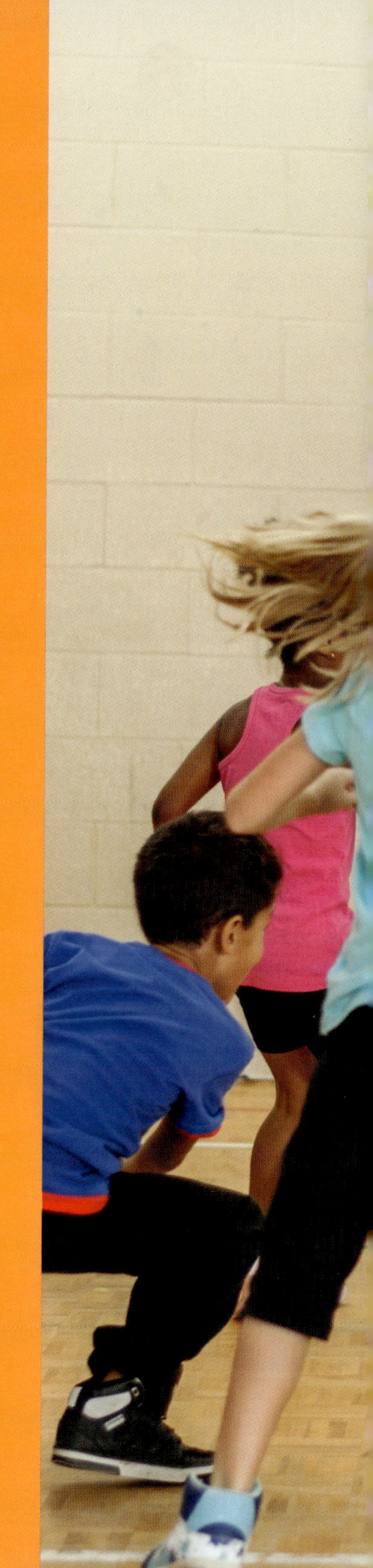

13

Mark shoots. He scores a basket.

Two points!

Ali is **fouled**. She shoots a free throw. One more point!

17

Zach plays **defense**. He tries to get the ball.

Liam shoots from the

3-point line. He scores!

ПОЛІЦІЯ
СУСІ БАР
21

Basketball Shots

3-pointer

free throw

layup

slam dunk

Glossary

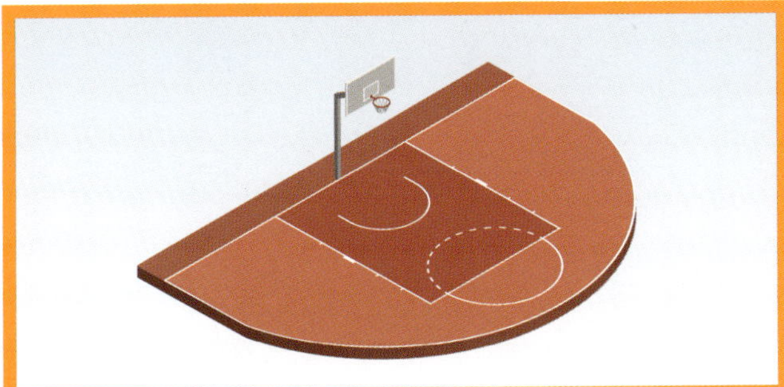

3-point line

a line on a basketball court 22 feet from the basket that earns players 3 points.

defense

the players of a team who try to stop the other team's offense from scoring.

fouled

illegally touched by another player.

Index

Visit **abdokids.com** and use this code to access crafts, games, videos, and more!